MONSTER TRUCKS
CAR CRUSHERS AND CROWD PLEASERS

Photography by Michael Bargo

Motorbooks International ®
Publishers & Wholesalers Inc

First published in 1986 by Motorbooks International Publishers & Wholesalers Inc, PO Box 2, 729 Prospect Avenue, Osceola, WI 54020 USA

Printed and bound in Hong Kong

The information in this book is true and complete to the best of our knowledge. All recommendations are made without any guarantee on the part of the author or publisher, who also disclaim any liability incurred in connection with the use of this data or specific details

Library of Congress Cataloging-in-Publication Data
Bargo, Michael.
    Monster trucks.
      1. Trucks—Miscellanea. I. Title.
TL230.B283 1986 796.7 86-12775
ISBN 0-87938-221-X

Motorbooks International books are also available at discounts in bulk quantity for industrial or sales-promotion use. For details write to Special Sales Manager at the Publisher's address

We recognize that many of the truck names used in this book belong to and are copyrighted by their owners. We use them for reference purposes only, and we are grateful for permission to do so.

Acknowledgments

The photos in this book were taken at exhibitions held by various motorsports promoters. Without their cooperation it would not have been possible to photograph the dramatic stunts and action photos. Among them are Chris Fritz, Steve Wood and Mike Mathis of United Sports of America; Neal Darnell of Main Attraction Promotions; George Carpenter of Standing Room Only; The United Hot Rod Association; and Susan Davis of The Promotion Company. Ross Fischer and Gary Rothrock of McCord Tire also supplied valuable contacts. Fred Shafer of Bearfoot, Inc., also provided valuable contacts and was extremely cooperative in performing daring stunts used in this book.

Cover photograph: Archetypal monster truck is *Samson I.* Owner Don Maple started with a 1984 Chevy Silverado, doubled up the frame and installed a blown 454 bored to 513 and added Rockwell axles. That simple; well, no, not really. Beautiful work, however you look at it.

Page 1: Monster truck chassis and drivetrains rely heavily on this sort of equipment. *Bearfoot's* five-ton Rockwell military axle shows how it's done. Four-wheel steering, heavyweight construction and "monster" power require this sort of strength.

Title page: "For your pleasure." At a show's opening the trucks are brought out for the national anthem and to introduce the drivers. Arrowhead Stadium for the United Sports of America sponsored show. All five trucks here are detailed in this book.

Opposite: Done crushing. Many junkyards enjoy the publicity in sponsoring cars ready for crushing.

Contents

Motionless and smoking, *Bigfoot* blows its torque converter in Indianapolis mud bog run. Sad but true.

The Monster Truck Phenomenon

It's halftime, and the truck-pulling competition has stopped for half an hour while the pullers prepare for the next round. Many of the stadium's 45,000 fans have left their seats and are at the concessions stands, ordering beer, hot dogs and popcorn.

Suddenly a thunderous roar is heard from the end of the stadium. The fans turn their heads to watch the pickup truck with tires over six feet tall and three feet wide roll onto the field toward a pile of junkyard cars. Sales at the stands stop, as everyone is waiting to see what will happen. The truck accelerates toward the cars, then slowly creeps up to them, touching them with its front tires. Then the truck backs up, and with an explosion of noise and energy, runs into the cars, the front end leaping into the air. Almost at the same instant, the rear tires hit the cars, thrusting the entire truck into the air like a horse kicking on its hind legs.

The driver of the truck lets his foot off the gas pedal, and the engine becomes eerily silent. The truck seems to float in the air, as though the driver were a magician and it is his willpower alone that keeps it aloft. For what seems like several seconds, the truck is standing still in an almost vertical position, its 14,000 lb. mass becoming almost weightless. Just when the crowd is mesmerized by this awesome spectacle, the truck begins to tilt forward and crashes down on the automobiles, crushing them. The engine roars again, like a defiant animal having shown its strength, and gently rolls off the cars.

As the crowd roars with approval, the truck circles around and spins all four tires as it does a donut in the dirt. This truck is called *Bearfoot* and its owner and driver, Fred Shafer, stops to wave to the crowd and open the tilt hood of the truck. Then he revs up the engine and crushes the cars again, this time approaching from the opposite side.

Bearfoot was the first truck to wheelstand while crushing cars, but this feat is performed at over a dozen locations around the country every weekend. What started with Bob Chandler's *Bigfoot*, the first monster truck, has grown to where there are now over 125 "monsters" around the country, although only two dozen or so are capable of consistently putting on a good show. The term "monster truck" was first used about 1982, when *Bigfoot, Bearfoot*, and *King Kong* were the only trucks that performed widely.

It's easy to determine if a truck fits the monster description: Most have the huge Terra or Firestone tires, and use the enormous 2 1/2 ton or five-ton Rockwell military steering axles. Some of the trucks in this book have huge tires that are not Terras, and the axles may not be Rockwells, but their size qualifies them as monster trucks.

The monster truck became a generic term and permanent part of the motorsports scene when *Four Wheeler* magazine published its first Monster Truck special issue in 1983. Since then, the toy industry has marketed dozens of monster truck models. *Bigfoot* and *Bearfoot* have appeared in films, made-for-TV movies and television. *Bearfoot* has even appeared in a rock video. Many big promoters regularly feature monster trucks as show pieces in their motocross competition, truck and tractor pulling, and mud bogging. County fairs across the country also feature them, and the Monster Corral has become a regular feature at the biggest off-road meet of the year, Petersen's *4-Wheel & Off-Road* Jamboree held in Indianapolis, Indiana, every September.

This book was produced to enable readers to share in the excitement, beauty and power of monster trucks. Not all of the excellent monster trucks are included, scheduling and space limitations did not allow me to feature them all. This collection of monster truck photographs is, however, the largest — and the variety of stunts featured is the greatest — yet published.

Barbarian I

Preceding pages
With its huge Firestone tractor tires mounted on 20 inch wheels, *Barbarian I* easily climbs over cars. *Barbarian I* is powered by a Chevy 454 engine, with a Predator carburetor, 560 duration Competition camshaft and Torker aluminum intake manifold. Power is fed to a Turbo 400 transmission and another three-speed auxiliary. The transfer case is a 2½ ton standard monster model. *Barbarian's* body is a 1978 Ford Ranger. It's unusual in that it uses a Chevy engine. The paint is black with gold flake, and it features several barbarians on the sides. It also has a Smittybilt triple roll bar, and six Stewart Warner lights on top. *Barbarian I's* front axle is a five-ton military with four shocks over each wheel. It also has custom-made springs and hydraulic torsion bars. The nylon ropes help keep the axle under control and limit spring extension. Rear axle is a Rockwell five-ton military, with four shocks over each wheel and custom-made springs.

Fred Shafer's Chevy-powered GMC *Bearfoot* is the best performing of all monster trucks. The height and quickness of his car-crushing wheelstands are awesome to watch. In this shot his rear tires are over a foot off the ground and his truck is high into the air.

Bearfoot IV

Bearfoot IV was built for Hollywood. It's going to be in a made-for-TV movie scheduled to be filmed in the Bahamas. It incorporates Fred Shafer innovations — the use of a Corvette differential on top to cut down drivetrain angle and planetary gears in the hubs — that have been copied by other monster trucks. The tailgate is finished in chrome. Two aluminum wheels extend to create a wheelie-bar, since Bearfoot often stands on end while pulling sleds or car crushing.

Fred Shafer with *Bearfoot*. Through Fred's ingenuity, *Bearfoot* has reached new heights of mechanical innovation and performance.

Following pages
Bearfoot is powered by a 454 big-block Chevy engine, with a 671 blower, and dual Holley carbs. It delivers about 850 horsepower.

Bearfoot uses five-ton Rockwell military axles, a 2½ ton International transfer case and Turbo 400 transmission to power its huge Terra tires. Its frame is heavily reinforced. Driveshaft u-joints are shielded to protect spectators from mechanical failure. There are four Burbank shocks per wheel.

Chuck and Fred unload the *Baby Bearfoot* off the trailer before a show. Fred wears a bear costume and does wheelstands with the *Baby* to the cheers of crowds around the country.

Bearfoot does a series of wheelstand car crushing in Kansas City's Arrowhead Stadium.

Bigfoot I & II

Preceding pages
Bigfoot tears through the mud bog, with its Alan Root custom-built Ford 460 engine bored to 640, a powerplant that delivers over 1000 horsepower. The all-aluminum engine has an 871 supercharger, three Predator carburetors, specially built aluminum intake manifold, planetary gears in the Case axles, hardened axle shafts and Ford C6 automatic transmission. It also has a 2½ ton international transfer case and five-ton Rockwell axles.

Two *Bigfoot* trucks are in this photo: *Bigfoot I* with the huge ten-foot tires, and *Bigfoot II* parked on top of it. *Bigfoot I* has a Ford 460 engine bored to 490, 671 blower and Predator carbs. This is fed to a Ford C6 automatic transmission, Case planetary axles and hardened axle shafts. There will be eight *Bigfoot* trucks built by the end of this year to satisfy the demand for *Bigfoot* at exhibitions around the country. Owner Bob Chandler.

Following pages
Bigfoot I looks like a giant roller skate with its ten-foot tires.

Crimson Giant's hood tilts, and it has a custom interior. It's powered by a 454 Chevy engine, with a 671 blower, two Predator carburetors, Holley electric fuel pump, and Eagle headers. The engine is kept lubricated by a Moroso deep-sump chrome oil pan and Moroso oil pump. Power is fed to a Chevy 400 manual transmission with chromed B&M deep transmission pan. Then it's routed to a 2½ ton Rockwell military transfer case to the two, five ton Rockwell axles.

Following pages

Crimson Giant is built from a 1974 Chevy ¾ ton frame and body. It's 12 feet high, weighs 12,000 pounds, and was built by Marvin Smith of Arnold, Missouri. The *Crimson Giant* easily crushes cars as it climbs over them at a show in Fort Smith, Arkansas. It was painted by Steve's Auto Body in Arnold, Missouri, and features a hand-painted *"Crimson Giant"* logo. The front end is embellished with a Warn 8000 pound winch mounted on a chrome Reflexion front bumper. *Crimson Giant*'s tailgate is beautifully painted and features a chrome Reflexion rear bumper. One of the two spun-aluminum ten-gallon tanks can be seen in this photo. It also has two, 3½ inch chrome roll bars and five KC lights. The rear axle is a triple-shocked five-ton Rockwell military axle. It is steered hydraulically. It's mounted on seven-leaf springs custom made by St. Louis Springs. The front axle is another Rockwell five-ton military mounted on seven-leaf springs. The underframe was custom built by the owner, Marvin Smith. Extra strength is needed to support the 957 pound Terra tires.

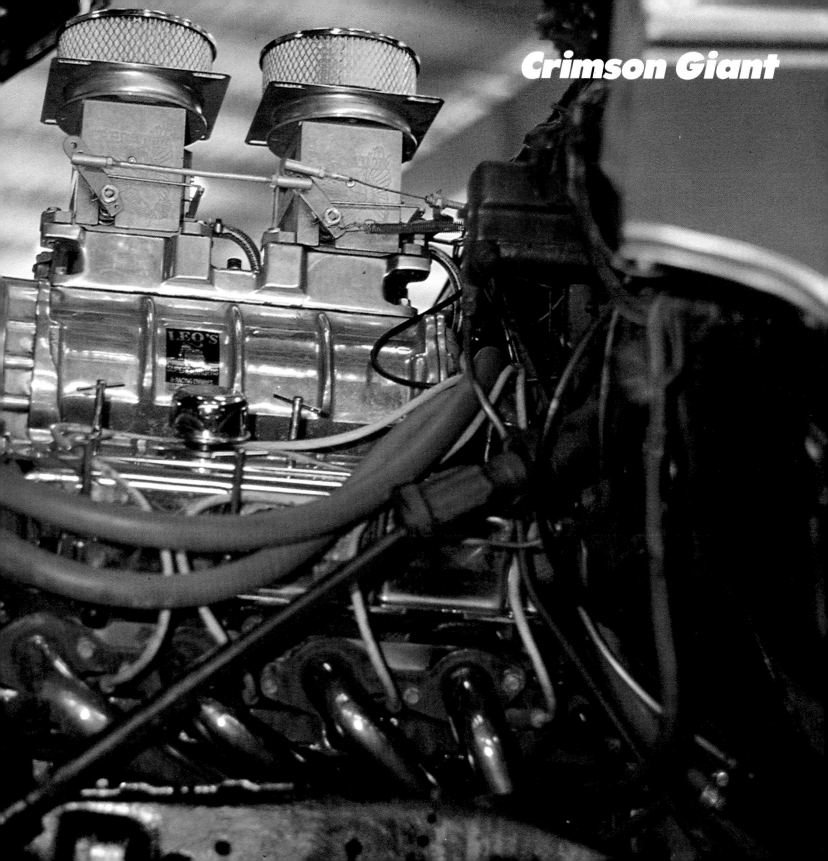

Crimson Giant

Preceding pages

Four exposures reveal how *Crimson Giant* climbs over cars.

Gentle Ben at the fall 1985 Indianapolis Petersen's *4-Wheel & Off-Road* Jamboree. The owner and builder, Kevin Presnell, brought along several animals with his truck, including his two bears Bo and Ceiphus.

Gentle Ben I

Gentle Ben was built on a 1972 Chevy Cheyenne Super 20 body. It has a 484 Chevy engine with dual 660 cfm Holley carburetors. This power is routed via a Chevy Turbo 400 transmission to two transfer cases: a New Process 205 and a 2½ ton Rockwell military. The suspension is made up of custom leafs by Warner Springs and 16 Rancho shock absorbers. It's 12½ feet tall and weighs 15,000 pounds.

The rear axle is a five-ton Rockwell military steering axle with four shocks over each Firestone tire. *Gentle Ben I* is braked by a disc brake system on the driveshafts, the style used by truck pullers. A massive tow bar allows *Ben* to pull sleds at exhibitions. The front axle features another five-ton Rockwell military axle, with four shocks over each Firestone tire. Steering is hydraulic. Lift is achieved with a combination of lift blocks and springs with 12 inches of arc.

Gentle Ben I is a favorite at car-crush exhibitions around the country, where its weight and power easily smash cars. There are two *Gentle Ben* trucks. *Gentle Ben I*, shown here, is the Chevy version. *Gentle Ben II* is built on a Ford Lariat body.

Godzilla's front axle reveals its custom framework. Steering gear and frame are beautifully painted. *Godzilla*'s front bumper is chrome-plated diamond plate, with two Warn Ox winches installed.

Godzilla is powered by a 653 cubic inch Detroit Diesel Allison engine. It puts out 1850 ft-lb of torque at 4000 rpm. Modifications include advanced cam timing, special fuel injectors and a "jake brake" to open the engine valves. Power is then routed via a six-speed Allison MT42 automatic transmission with a heavy-duty torque converter. It then is fed to a Timkin T-77 transfer case to its two driveshafts. *Godzilla*'s suspension and axles include five-ton Rockwell military steering axles, 15 inch lift towers, re-arched springs with rebound leaves, 5½ inch spring hangers and four Rancho shock absorbers at each wheel. *Godzilla*'s custom paint job is one of the best on any monster truck. This includes the gold Godzilla sign on the door and several murals located on the hood and sides of cargo box. The tilt bed reveals beautifully painted frame, four Rancho shocks on each wheel, and chrome-plated 32x38 inch wheels. One side of *Godzilla*'s tilt bed shows the "Godzilla" monster crushing cars and a bus with its feet. With the tilt bed up, *Godzilla* stands over 16 feet tall! With a weight of 20,000 pounds, it's also one of the heaviest monster trucks.

Godzilla at the September 1985 Petersen's *4-Wheel & Off-Road* magazine's Jamboree Nationals. A large crowd gathered around the truck for three days, with owner Al Thurber and son selling novelties.

A small radio-controlled version of *Godzilla*, complete with huge tires and paint job, do car-crushing stunts for the crowd.

Goliath

Alan Tura's *Goliath* is the first twin-engined monster truck. It easily glides over cars as it wheelstands in Springfield, Illinois. *Goliath*'s rear axle is a 15,000 pound Clarke planetary from heavy equipment. There's another Dana 60 differential mounted on top to decrease driveshaft angle and increase strength. It has Rugged Trail Monster shocks, airbags and a custom-made lift kit using blocks. The springs are modified military springs with ten leaves. It uses McCord wheels and 66″ Super Terra Grip tires. The *Goliath* logo was beautifully painted in *Flintstones* style by Guy Shively. The body was painted a mariner Imron blue by Maaco in Youngstown, Ohio. *Goliath*'s body and chrome work are as beautifully finished as any monster's. It has a Holbrecht double chrome roll bar, Reflexion rear bumper and 14 KC Daylighter lights.

Goliath's unique second engine is mounted in the pickup bed. Each engine is a 1969 Ford 460 bored to 472. They have 8.5:1 compression; Arias forged flat top pistons; TRW C1-77 bearings; Holley aluminum valve covers; Crane camshaft, pushrods and springs; and a Cloyes true double-roller timing chain. TRW valves, Hedman headers, 2″ exhaust pipes and Holley electric fuel pumps are some of the high-performance accessories that enable the engines to put out 1000 horsepower each.

The truck features a tilt body similar to *USA-1*. Before and after shows, Scott lifts the body up for the crowd. *King Krunch* uses the Firestone 23 tire, similar to the Terra and 66 inches tall. With bed lifted up, spectators can view all the components that make *King Krunch* a superb performer. It's powered by a Chevy 454 bored to 468, with a Weiand tunnel ram, two Predator carbs, Competition camshaft and hooker headers. Power is then fed to a TCI custom-modified Turbo 400 transmission, 2½ ton Rockwell military transfer case and five-ton Rockwell military axles.

The painting was done by Pee Wee's of Spring, Texas, and the roll bar was made by Stull Industries. Front axle uses springs taken from a Mack truck and custom built 10x4 inch frame. There are four Trailmaster shocks over each wheel. Rear axle uses Mack truck springs, five-ton Rockwell axle and four Trailmaster shocks on each wheel.

Following pages
King Krunch is one of the more popular monsters on the circuit. It's built on a 1985 Silverado body. It becomes airborne when it crushes cars.

King Krunch

Knight Stalker

Knight Stalker uses its big-block Ford to crush cars at the spring 1986 Petersen's Jamboree.

Front axle features burgundy-painted Monroe series 70 shocks, the largest commercially available, and Rockwell five-ton axle.

While many monster trucks have stock interiors, *Knight Stalker*'s is beautifully finished.

Following pages

Knight Stalker is built from a 1979 Ford Lariat F250 pickup. It has a ten-inch Ford truck frame, and is powered by a Ford 460 motor. The motor has 7:1 pistons and Sig-Erson Cam, and puts out 600 horsepower. This power is routed through a modified C6 transmission, then two transfer cases: a New Process 205, and 2½ REO truck transfer case. It is a beautifully painted truck with *Knight Stalker* murals. It was painted by TS Customs of Waterford, Wisconsin. Front and rear bumpers were custom made by the owner, who also did the frame modification work.

Kodiak

Preceding pages
At the spring 1986 Petersen's Jamboree *Kodiak* ran the obstacle for the fans.

Mark Bendler's *Kodiak* is one of the most heavily built and beautiful monsters. At the spring 1986 Jamboree, fans crowd around the truck to view its unusual construction. *Kodiak*'s double frame is over two feet high and makes it virtually bulletproof. *Kodiak* is built from a 1980 Chevrolet body, with a 454 bored to 496. High engine performance is achieved with an Edelbrock tunnel ram, two 660 Holley carburetors and Brodix aluminum heads. A view of *Kodiak*'s rear axle shows its unique "drop box" direct-chain drive to reduce the driveshaft angle. This feeds power to a Pettibone axle with 140 ton planetary gears in the hubs. There are 28 Rugged Trail shock absorbers over the 20 ton military leaf springs. The front axle is another steering axle with the same shocks and leaf springs. The drop box is located under the cab so it won't get in the way during car crushes.

Kodiak's Chevy 496 engine provides the power to take it over cars. A 60 ton hydraulic winch up front provides the power needed to pull the monster out of any muck that might bog down the Firestone tires. The winch was originally used in a Milwaukee utility company line truck.

The front axle has Rugged Trail shocks, military leaf springs and a Pettibone heavy-equipment steering axle. *Kodiak*'s massive frame, bigger than most monsters', provides the strength needed to carry the heavy axles and tires over cars. *Kodiak*'s engine power is routed via a Chevy Turbo 400 transmission with 3500 rpm B & M torque converter to a five-speed manual transmission.

Little Bearfoot

Little Bearfoot is powered by a Chevy 454 bored to 460 cubic inches, blown with Holley carburetors. It's run by a 2½ ton military transfer case, Chevy Turbo 400 transmission and five-ton Rockwell axles. It was the first "high-tech" monster. It uses two differentials on the axles: a Corvette rear end on top to cut down on the driveshaft angle, and the differential in the five-ton Rockwell axle. Another innovation was the use of planetary gears in the hubs. The little 1982 S-10 body could fit four Terra tires, a remarkable achievement considering the weight and bulk of the tires. To make the truck strong enough, Fred used two frames: a Chevy one-ton crew cab frame with the S-10 pickup's frame welded inside. The truck's owner, builder and driver, Fred Shafer, was responsible for many of the mechanical innovations that made today's high-performance monsters a reality. At a Fourth of July celebration in St. Louis, *Little Bearfoot* crushed six cars simultaneously, with its duals mounted.

Spectators marvel at the enormous amount of rubber used to make *Little Bearfoot* the monster with the widest footprint. Each Goodyear Terra tire is 74 inches tall. *Little Bearfoot* was one of the first monster trucks to have a thematic mural painted on the truck body.

Lone Eagle

Lone Eagle does a 360 degree spin in the dirt for the crowd.

Front axle of *Lone Eagle* with Trail Master shocks, Rockwell axle and custom traction bar. Rear axle features u-joint guards, Trail Master shocks and five-ton Rockwell axle.

Lone Eagle easily crushes cars with its 468 Chevy big-block, 13.5:1 TRW pistons, roller cam, tunnel ram and two Predator carbs. It has 800 horsepower, enough to get it airborne. *Lone Eagle* is built from a 1984 K30 Chevy Silverado pickup body. *Lone Eagle*'s rear axle is a Rockwell five-ton with Detroit Locker differential. There's a disc brake on the driveshaft. It has four Trail Master shocks over each wheel and Warn hubs.

Lone Eagle is beautifully painted and finished. It features a Winch Master front bumper, KC Day-lighters, 66 inch tall Firestone tires and aluminum wheels from Off-Road Specialties, an off-road shop that's also the home of *USA-1*. *Lone Eagle*'s tilting bed features a triple double-roll bar, KC Daylighters and Reflexion rear bumper.

Master of Disaster

Master of Disaster makes easy work of crushing cars with its 66 inch tall tires. They're cushioned by 12 Rancho shocks — three on each wheel. Doug Spanier of Albany, Minnesota, is owner and builder of *Master of Disaster.* He tours with the United Sports of America promoters all around the country. *Master of Disaster*'s mural is copied off of the *Molly Hatchet* album cover of the same name. It's the most beautifully painted door mural on any monster truck. *Master of Disaster* features some interior luxuries: a Bose stereo, six-way power seats and electric doors — there are no door handles, it opens with the touch of a button!

Master of Disaster climbs atop some cars at Kansas City's Arrowhead Stadium. It's based on a 1984 Chevy pickup body, with a Chevy 454 engine. With its single Predator carburetor it puts out 450 horsepower. This power is fed through a Chevrolet Turbo 400 transmission, then a two-ton GMC transfer case to the five-ton Rockwell military axles.

Master of Disaster broke part of its front axle during a car crush — not unusual for a monster truck — and had to be helped off the field by a payloader. Next day a welder repaired the job in the pit area. The front axle features a disc brake on the driveshaft and three Rancho shocks over each wheel of the five-ton Rockwell axle.

Michigan Ice Monster

Brett, holding the helmet, discusses the *Ice Monster*'s performance after running an obstacle course. The *Ice Monster* performs around the country doing car crushing, exhibitions and whatever other stunts the promoters can invent for Brett. *Ice Monster* has beautifully designed and painted artwork. Its huge 66 inch Terra tires and doubled-up frame give it the strength to crush cars week after week. The front axle has a doubled-up frame and six Trailmaster nitrogen gas shocks on each wheel.

Ice Monster's rear axle has traction bars, re-arched springs and six shocks over each wheel. Both front and rear axles are the Rockwell five-ton military variety. The front axle has a doubled-up frame and six Trailmaster nitrogen gas shocks on each wheel. The *Ice Monster* was created at the Great Lakes Four-wheel-drive Center in Grand Rapids. It has achieved a reputation as a great-performing show truck. It's powered by a Chevy 454 bored to 460, Predator carburetion and Crower cam. This power is routed through a Turbo 350 transmission, New Process 205 transfer case and a five-ton military transfer case.

Michigan Ice Monster was built by Brett Engelman of Grand Rapids, Michigan, who also drives the monster at exhibitions. He did these stunts with the *Ice Monster* at Arrowhead Stadium in Kansas City, Missouri.

Orange Crush

Preceding pages

Orange Crush is a favorite whenever it appears in front of a crowd. It was built by Joe Gardner & Sons, of Waterloo, Iowa, and has unusually strong and heavy components. Its front axle is a ten-ton axle from earth-moving equipment. It has planetary gears at the hubs for great strength and hydraulic steering. *Crush*'s rear axle is a ten-ton axle used by earth-moving equipment, and the suspension incorporates lift blocks and Goodyear airbags. The airbags act both to limit spring travel and dampen shocks. Its driveshafts are beautifully finished and painted. The frame is reinforced with square steel tubing to both make the frame more rigid and protect drivetrain components from damage. Its tailgate and rear bumper are chromed and painted. Gold and a beautiful paint job highlight *Orange Crush*'s undercarriage. The five-ton military transfer case provides power to both driveshafts and is protected for car crushing.

The *Crush*'s tires are perhaps the biggest on any monster truck: They're 77 inches tall and weigh 996 pounds apiece. Made by Firestone, the tires are used by heavy equipment.

Following pages

At Kansas City's Arrowhead Stadium *Taurus* and *Orange Crush* were each chained to a car and pulled it apart. The car simply ripped in half. Its frame had not been cut or the body tampered with in any way. The stunt was sponsored by United Sports of America.

Renegade I is a solid performer at car crushes and exhibitions. The Chevy 454 engine, with 10:1 pistons, 850 Holley carb and Torker manifold provide plenty of power for car crushing.

Preceding pages
Renegade is built on one of the oldest truck bodies of any monster truck. *War Wagon* is one of the few that's older; it's a 1964 GMC pickup body.

Renegade used the mighty five-ton Rockwell axles, a heavy custom-made frame and huge 66 inch Terras. *Renegade*'s front axle shows its heavy axle, 14 inch lift blocks, red brake guards, truck springs and heavy framework. Rear axle is supported under a frame from a 2½ ton military truck shortened to fit the old GMC pickup body. Propeller gives the illusion that *Renegade* can travel in water.

Samson I

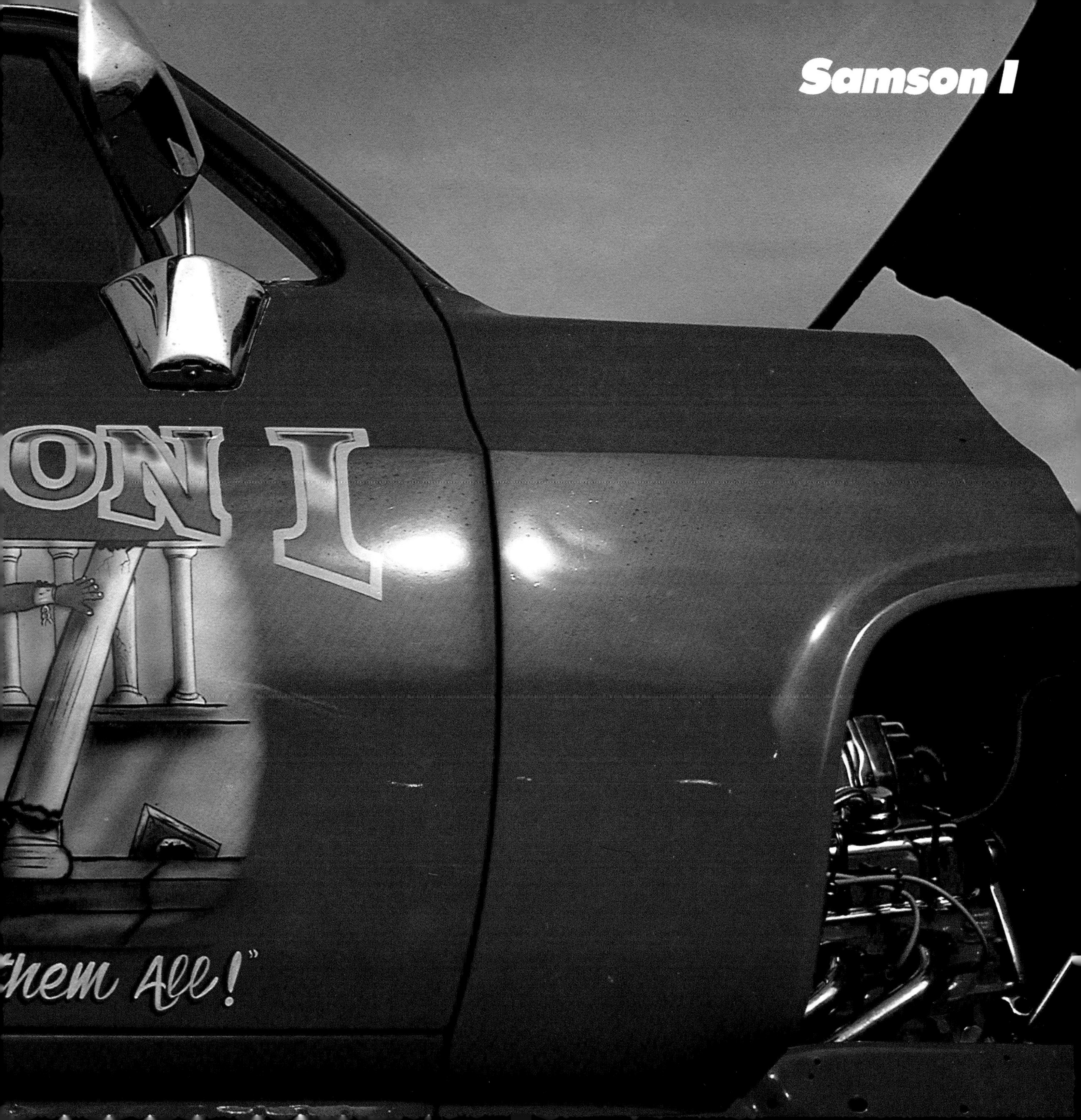

Preceding pages
Samson's Biblical roots are displayed on the door's murals, "strongest of them all."

Samson I uses four chromed roll bars for protection. So much of a monster truck's weight is in the frame and axles, however, that a rollover is very unlikely.

Following pages
Owner Don Maple checks out his Chevy engine: It puts out almost 1000 horsepower! With the hood raised, *Samson I* shows its doubled-up framework and blown Chevy 454 bored out to 513.

Samson I's axles are beautifully painted and chromed. They're the five-ton Rockwell military steering axles, reinforced with P251 planetary gears at the hubs, taken from a US Army payloader for great strength, an innovation first used by *Little Bearfoot. Samson*'s great strength is routed through a Turbo 400 transmission, heavily modified to take the extra horsepower and torque, then distributed to both driveshafts through a New Process 203 transfer case coupled to a five-ton military transfer case.

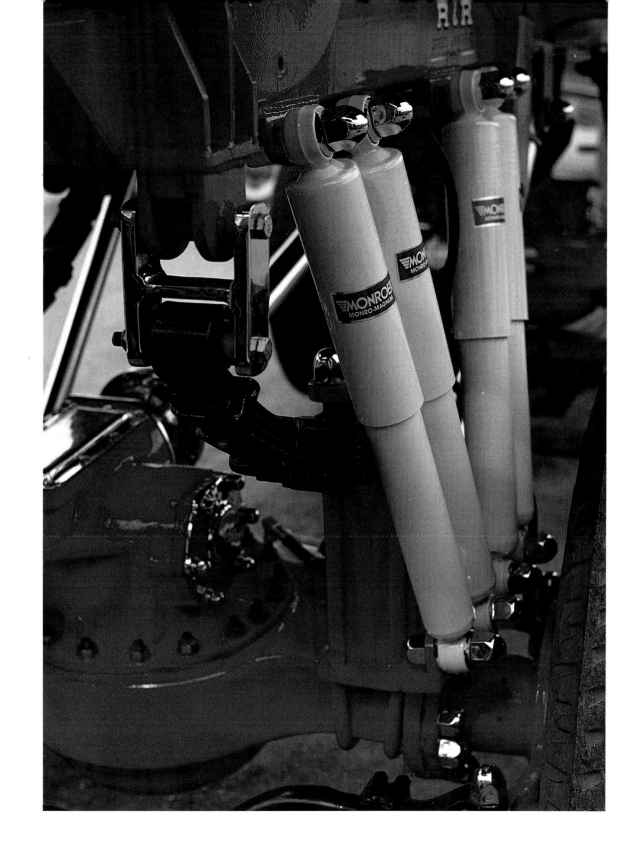

Showtime was built by Brian Shell, a truck painter and auto body shop manager in Fraser, Michigan. His attention to fine detail and workmanship show in his axles and body painting work. Brian's engine is not only a thing of beauty but of power: It's a Ford 460 bored out to 514 cubic inches, Hampton supercharged, with nitrous oxide and Holley 660 carburetors. It also has forged-true pistons, a Crane cam and a 12 quart oil system. It delivers 946 horsepower at 6400 rpm. This power is fed via a Ford C 6 transmission, modified by Bill's Transmission in Roseville, Michigan. Then it's routed through a New Process 204 transfer case, followed by a 2½ ton military transfer case. The engine work was done by Total Performance in Mount Clemen, Michigan, by the owner, John Vermeersch. He is a consultant for Ford Motorsport.

Showtime uses five-ton Rockwell military axles, 24 Rugged trail shocks, and five-ton military springs arched 22 inches by D & W in Detroit. *Showtime's* tires are the 73 inch tall Firestone tires. Wheels are custom made by McCord Tire of Monticello, Indiana, and are 38x32 inch custom modulars. Brian's tailgate shows the attention and work given to detailing the truck. Other features include hydraulic-tilt front end, smoked glass and lower door handles. It also has an Eagle three-inch roll bar. *Showtime* is 14 feet tall and weighs 18,000 pounds! The hand-built frame was made from 2x6x¼ tubing, with some parts made from 2x2x¼ and 3x3x¼. All mounts were custom made and fit from steel stock.

Southern Sunshine

Views of *Southern Sunshine* show custom murals and body work. *Southern Sunshine's* front axle is a massive Pettibone axle taken from a cherry-picker. Springs were picked up "from a junkyard," according to the builder. Two big shocks dampen each wheel's travel. Rear axle is another Pettibone from a cherry-picker, with springs salvaged from a junkyard. Two shocks are installed over each wheel, and frame is a heavily reinforced ladder type.

At 15,000 pounds, *Southern Sunshine* is one of the heaviest monsters with its Pettibone cherry-picker axles. It easily crushes cars with the huge 66x43x25 Firestone tires. *Southern Sunshine* is built on a Chevy Silverado body, painted white with custom red, yellow and orange stripes. It's powered by a Chevy 454 with a Holley 650 double pumper. The quivering includes a 2½ ton military transfer case and Turbo 400 transmission.

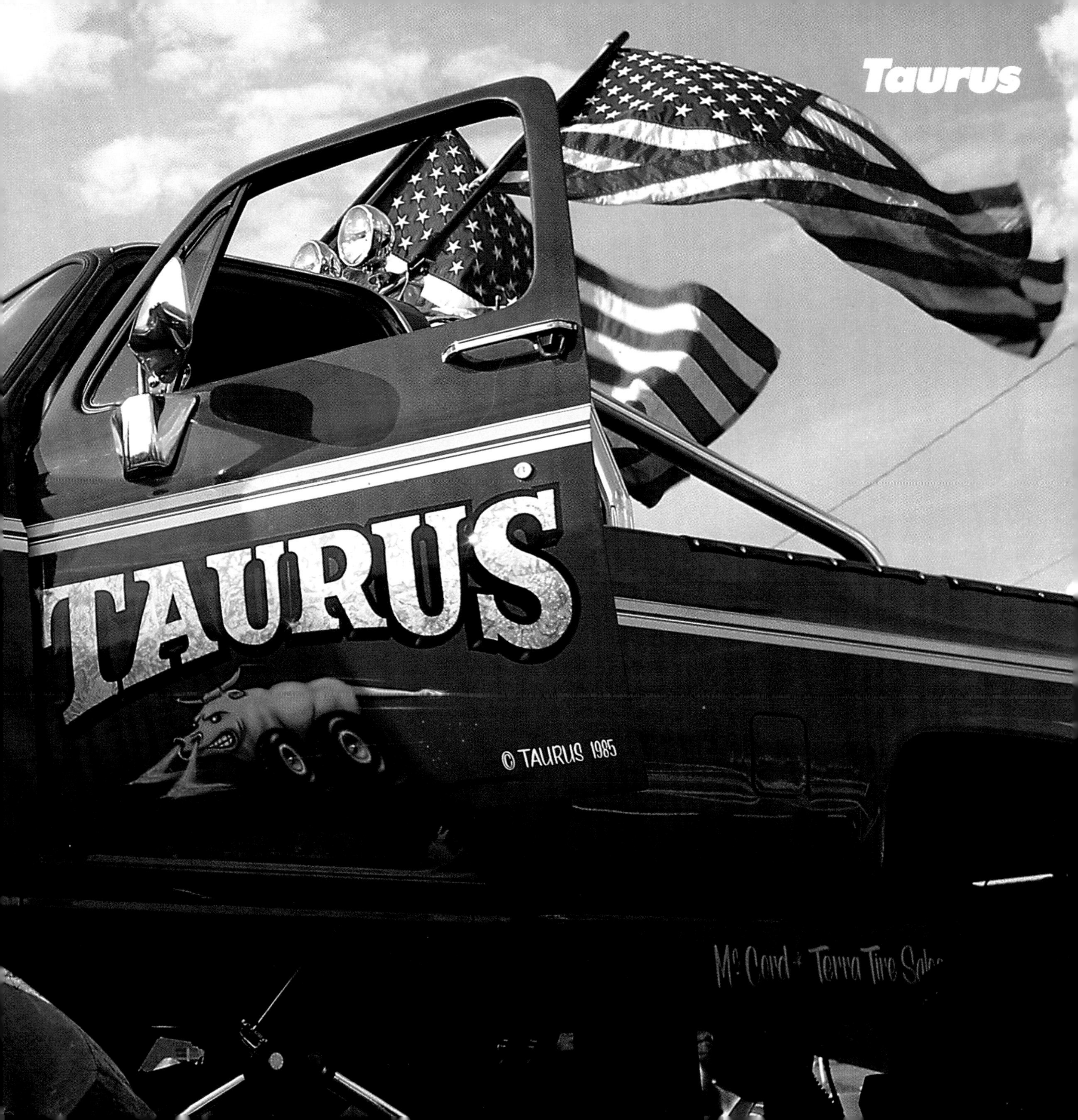
TAURUS
© TAURUS 1985

Taurus has the huge 74 inch tall Goodyear Terra tires. *Taurus'* big-block Chevy engine is one of the most powerful of any monster's, using a sophisticated gasoline-injected, blown system. It has 671 Hillborn injection feeding a 6.71 blower with ten percent overdrive, developing 1200 horsepower.

Seen in profile, the 1986 Chevy K20 pickup body blends perfectly with the large tires and wheels.

Taurus easily crushes cars with its huge tires and 1200 horsepower blown, fuel-injected Chevy engine.

Following pages

The axles are five-ton Rockwell military style, with Huff payloader planetary gears in the hubs for added strength. Each wheel has four Trail Master shocks, totaling 16. The u-joints of the truck are shielded as they leave the 2½ ton, New Process 203 transfer case.

113

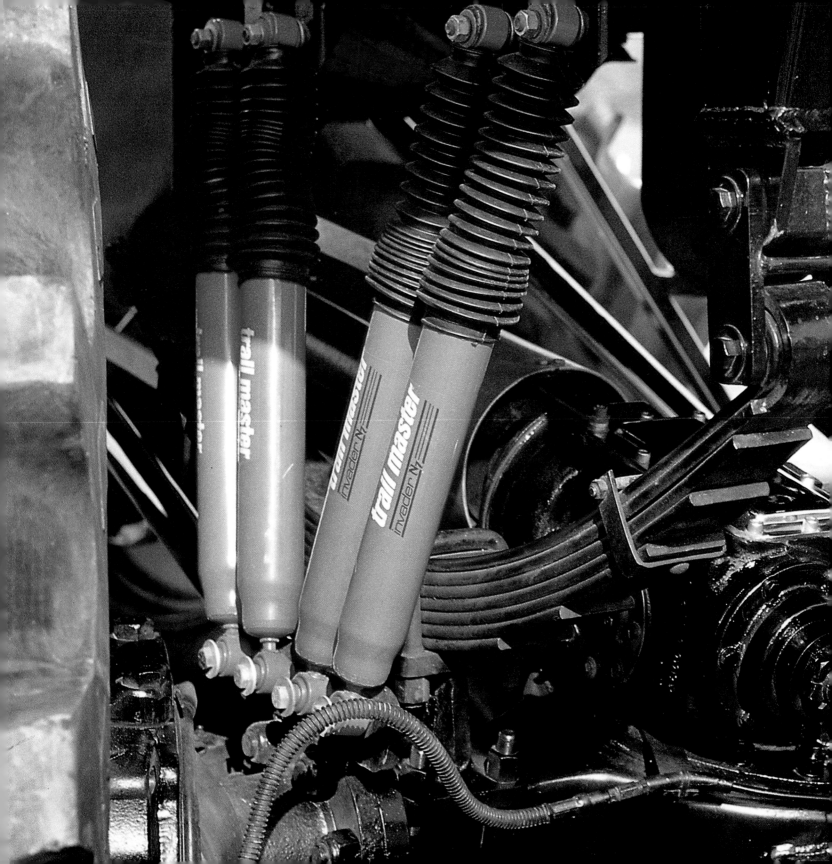

USA-1

Preceding pages
USA-1 is one of the oldest monsters and best performers. It's been on television's *That's Incredible* and *Battle of the Monster Trucks.* It often performs with Bob Chandler's *Bigfoot.* Currently, *USA-1* is sponsored by Pennzoil and True-Value Master Mechanics tools. *USA-1* was the first popular monster to have a hydraulically lifted body. It's an eye catcher at truck pulls and mud bogging competitions where *USA-1* often appears as an exhibition vehicle. *USA-1* also sports a four-inch custom-made chrome roll bar and six KC Daylighters. A Deist flame-out fire extinguishing system is plumbed throughout the vehicle for added protection.

USA-1's engine is a Chevy 454 bored to 540. It runs on nitrous oxide, with Predator carburetion, Competition camshaft and valvetrain, Hedman headers and MSD ignition. This power is routed through a Turbo 400 transmission to a Rockwell 223 transfer case.

USA-1's entire pickup body tilts upward to reveal its engine and suspension details. It's built on a 1970 Chevy ½ ton body, with a Warn winch up front, chrome bumper and four Rugged Trail shocks on each wheel. There's also two Rugged Trail steering stabilizers on the front axle. Each axle is the five-ton Rockwell, with custom-made springs, Detroit Locker differential and Warn locking hubs. Lift blocks and frame were custom-made for *USA-1*.

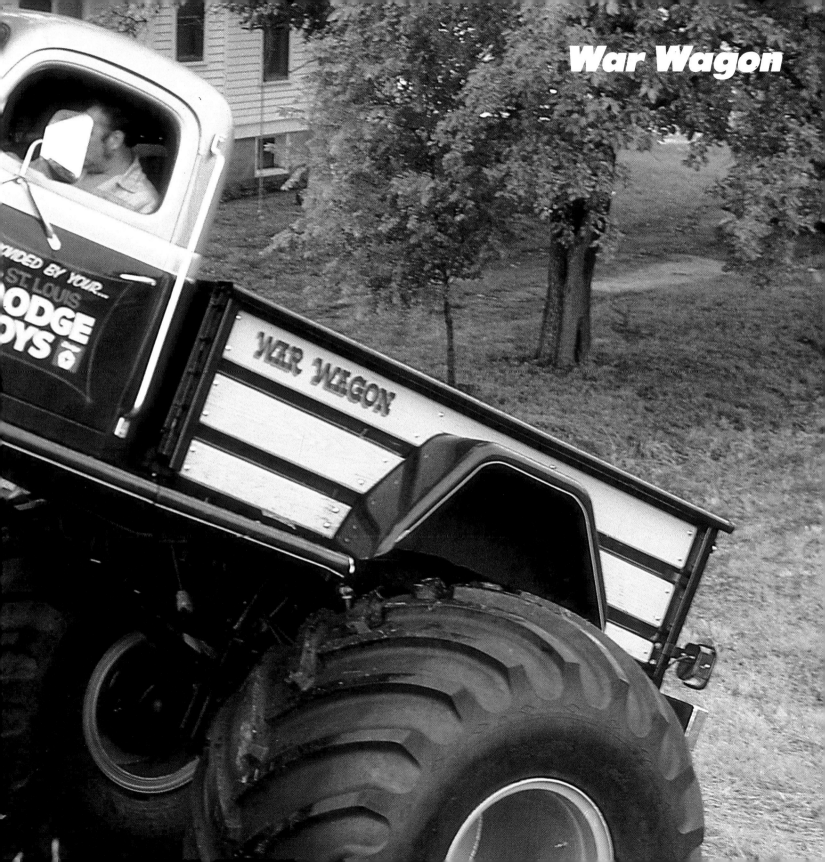

War Wagon

Preceding pages

War Wagon is used strictly as an exhibition vehicle, and has been leased by St. Louis Dodge Dealers as a showpiece. But it can easily manage a Missouri levee!

War Wagon is one of the oldest monster trucks. It's based on a 1945 Dodge Power Wagon body. Owner Harold Arbeitman obtained it when he swapped a brand-new 1979 Dodge Power Wagon for it. The cab is original, but the bed was taken from a 1972 Dodge. It's had custom-made fenders added, hand-made wooden platform, tailgate accents and box accents. The bumpers are custom made and sleekly chromed, with a Warn winch up front, a chrome tube grille guard and chromed grille. The smaller 2½ Rockwell military axles are used on the truck to support its 66 inch tall tires. Both axles steer. The springs were taken from a Dodge semi-tractor, and are supplemented with hand-built lift blocks, stabilizer bars and two Rough Country shocks on each wheel. It's 12 feet tall.

Following pages

War Wagon is powered by one of the classic motors of the 1960s: a 1967 Plymouth 426 hemi, with Ed Pink 6.71 blower, MT rods, a pair of twin Holleys and Isky roller-pushing Crane valves. Power is then fed to a 727 Loadflite transmission via a TCI torque converter, special Competition clutch packs and bands, and the original 1946 transfer case. The power is geared down by the 6.72 ratioed axles. Part-time Warn hubs enable Harold to use two-wheel drive.